JavaScript

js

Ming Li

Dedication

To all of you with the strong desire to learn
the scripting language JavaScript (js).
Having the desire to learn is the best to succeed.

Table Of Contents

1- <u>Who is it for?</u>

JavaScript is a very easy programming language to learn and excel at, it is used in parallel with HTML (Hyper Text Markup Language) and CSS (Cascading Style Sheet).

A basic knowledge of the 2 above helps you start right away with JavaScript programming. But don't be scared and don't you worry, having a great desire to learn is the key to success.

JavaScript is friendly to use and once you achieve the learning journey you'll be very happy accomplishing the success.

Start with the basic then each time you finish a level with full understanding you move your way up!

2- <u>Introduction and History:</u>

In early 1990s the web world was created but the pages in that time were static with no user interaction with the page.

That time 2 browsers were popular enough to be mentioned, Netscape that used the programming language and allowed the pages to become interactive, with no compilation needed to interpret the commands.

The other one was Java with its own plugin which got known soon enough that Netscape renamed its language to JavaScript.

Internet Explorer was updated as well to support the vscript and the Jscript which was quite similar to Javascript.

Once Internet Explorer topped the browsers JavaScript became the accepted standard for interaction.

JavaScript is Not Java programming language in fact it is so different they have different semantics. It is an easier language to learn, it facilitates the interaction with the user, it is very dynamic and very popular used by most web browsers nowadays.

It has many features that allow support of the object-oriented,

Developed by Brendan Eich of Netscape which is an internet, software and telecommunication industry, JavaScript a client side scripting language.

During its development JavaScript was called Mocha then LiveScript, Brendan Eich was trying to make it seams like the little brother of Java.

ECMAScript the scripting name got adjusted to JavaScript to avoid resemblance with skin disease.

The competing browsers took into consideration this scripting language and its continuous growth and in 1996 JavaScript became the responsibility of the international standards body ECMA to be developed and was officially named ECMAScript, but people refer to it as JavaScript.

It creates interactive effects as we will explain later on, it is supported by the major web browsers such as internet explorer and...

Any plain text editor such as Notepad can be used to code in JavaScript.

It is used with HTML Hyper Text Markup Language that is used to create static web pages. HTML is not a programming language but JavaScript is and its code is included in the HTML code sometimes, often developers use JavaScript in a separate file with a ".js" extension that should be saved in the same path or folder as the HTML one and that way it is much easier to modify the *js* file without having to check a heavy coding file.

And all what we have to do is link both of them by using the open/close Tags <script>...</script> and the slash is to end the tag similarly to an HTML ending tag.

The JavaScript then is added to as many pages as we need to of course with the appropriate JavaScript code.

Note:

If you use HTML5 then it is enough to use just <script> as an open tag.

If you use older than HTML5 then use <script type="text/javascript"> as an open tag.

If it is written for others to use on their own websites such as WordPress plugins etc use   <script type="text/javascript"> as well or use CDATA section if your document need to parse as XML and when you want to write something like i<20 instead of i<20 and

a && b instead of a&& b which is not a problem if the file source is externally stored.

Browser treating the markup as HTML then: <script>Your Code Here</script> if treated as XML then:

<script>

<![CDATA[

   ...Your code here

]]>

</script>

CDATA section tells the parser to not treat "<" and "&" as control characters.

The most used browsers are:

Internet Explorer, Google Chrome, Mozilla Firefox, Apple Safari and Opera.

You can enable JavaScript in your browser easily by following these steps:

Internet Explorer:

Open your browser as usual

Click on the wheel up corner with the home and star

Click on Internet options

Click on security then select Custom level at the bottom

Scroll down to Active scripting and check Enable

Click yes to the prompt then OK on the Internet Options menu

Refresh your browser by clicking on the arrow http://... area or hit F5 which is under View in the Menu Bar that you can get if missing from right click on Home symbol up right corner of the browser.

3- JavaScript definition:

JavaScript is a programming language that uses code which works behind the content of the web page you look at. So the user doesn't see what is behind the content of the page but the computer or the processor does.

However you can view the source code by right clicking on the page and choosing "view source code", yep you can view it!

HTML uses elements, it is a coding language somehow, it uses texts, paragraphs, links, images tags and much more to build a web page, CSS code styles it and gives it a better look by using selectors such as color, font, background-color and much more to those pages created in HTML, JavaScript take it farther by bringing dynamic to the page which without it is just a static one and could be boring, so it controls the page by making the interaction with the user possible and fun, when the user clicks on something.

4- JavaScript is a scripting Language:

JavaScript is included in the file used to create the web page, which is saved as .html file,

You don't need really a separate file to run JavaScript in that web page it runs within it.

But you can use a separate file to code in JavaScript with .js extension instead that makes it easy for future updates and corrections of the code.

Because it is a scripting language used to enhance the page that used HTML and CSS.

We call it an interpretive language, most instructions are executed directly, it is fast,easy and cost effective to use.

The compiled languages are complex because of the code compilation.

5- <u>Are JavaScript and Java the same?</u>

They are completely different, while JavaScript is a scripting language used with HTML and CSS, Java is not related to them and is a compiled language.

In the world of web development JavaScript is the one to use, the similarity in the name is just a marketing thing, when it was developed by Netscape in the 1990's Java was very popular and by calling it JavaScript it got easier to be known.

Netscape handed the language to ECMA which is a global company, since then all famous browsers did support the ECMAScript still called by everyone JavaScript..

6- <u>The start:</u>

To get started we need to do few things to be set and to make sure it is organized

So you will create a folder and save it somewhere you remember and which will hold all the files that you will create to learn JavaScript.

6a- <u>Folder creation:</u>

Creating web pages need many files to be saved in the same path, to get hold of them easily and also coding files have to be in the same place.

Let us create a file called Basic JavaScript, you have the choice to put it anywhere you want in you PC or mac.

- Windows: right click on an empty space and choose New-Folder then type in the name Basic JavaScript.

- <u>Mac OS</u>: CTRL + click an empty space and choose New Folder, click the new entitled folder, select it, click the untitled folder again, select the name and write "Basic JavaScript" press Enter.

- <u>Windows PC</u>: choose the path where you like to have your file then, right Click in an empty space, select New, then folder, left mouse Click to accept, once done, right click on the empty folder and Click Rename then type the file name you want.

Once the folder to keep the work is ready let's create a web page because JavaScript is created in it.

Let's use a plain Text Editor, Notepad for windows for example to code or anyone that you have.

Start with "<!DOCTYPE html>" tag which means that the document used is HTML.

The browser as well expects that.

1. let's use "Notepad (free), Notepad++ (free), TextEdit, KomodoEdit (free), Dreamweaver, TextWrangler (free) or any other you prefer..." to create a web page.

If ICloud used, put the folder you created in your hard drive.

Note: Change TextEdit preferences to plain text.

HTML Code file: HTML is not sensitive to lower and upper cases. Minimum tags needed to create a web page are:

<!DOCTYPE html>

<html> </html> are the open/close HTML tags between which all the coding will be.

<head> </head> the open/close that can have <title>....</title> open/close tags

<body> </body> open/close tags where paragraphs and maybe lists and other tags will be.

Summary of the code:

<!DOCTYPE html>
<html>
<head>

<title>name to your web page, when you google it will be found</title>

</head>

<body>

</body>

</html>

Notepad code file:

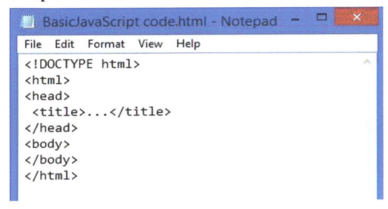

Choose File then Save or hit CTL + S for windows Notepad for example or save it the way you normally do.

If it is the first time you save it then you get the Save AS.

Save as type: choose All files & for File name: BasicJavaScript.html or htm this will work as well, find the folder BasicJavaScript you created to get organized and hit the Save button.

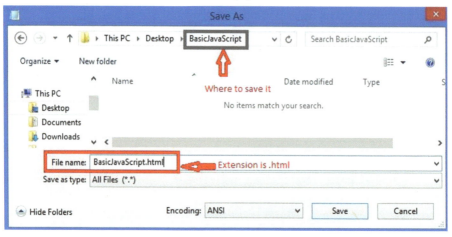

I used .html as extension.

For a Macintosh: when **Save As** opens type in the file name and search for the folder that you created to save it in as .html extension and hit the Save button.

Note:

To open the file code you created, right click on it , choose Open with, then choose the browser you want, I personally use Google Chrome.

Once opened with your choice of browser it will be blank, because it has only the minimum HTML code, without any content yet.

6b- Start coding in JavaScript:

Through examples you will learn JavaScript, you will type the code, understand its purpose and check its work once viewed in the browser, in a simple way and step by step.

Starting with the basic is always the best then build your way up to more advanced coding, this way you build the confidence to code in

JavaScript easily and be even creative.

1- HTML Tags: needed for JavaScript.

Open the file 'Basic JavaScript', I used Notepad (or another text editor you used), double click to open it.

So far we have only HTML tags, but go ahead and add the JavaScript code in it and to tell the browser where the start code and the end code are use the following open/close tags:

<script>

</script>

Script just means the scripting language.

So what comes after the opening script tag <scrip> is JavaScript, and after the closing tag </script> is not JavaScript language, no other coding type like HTML or CSS go in between those 2 tags.

Let's put them after the HTML's <body> tag.

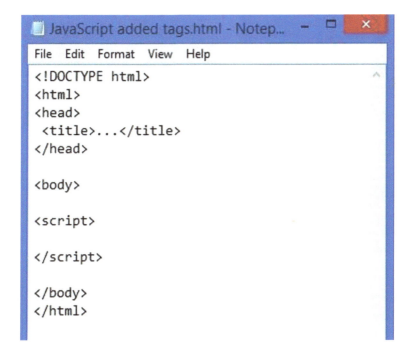

You might of seen:

<script type="text/javascript"> as an opening script tag.

</script> closing script tag.

This is used with XHTML which stands for Extensible Hyper Text Markup Language, which is slightly different than HTML and has strict rules to be followed, not like HTML in case you forgot a closing tag of a paragraph for example will still work.

Sometimes out of habit people they still use: type="text/javascript" which is fine to do so in HTML5 (the fifth revision of HTML with new elements).

You might of seen also this code which is no longer recommended

<script type = "text/javascript" language="javascript"> as an opening script tag.

</script> closing script tag.

7- JavaScript Comment:

// Single line JavaScript comment or use: /* to start and */ to end it.

/* Multiline JavaScript comment start & */ Multiline JavaScript comment end.

They should be used in the JavaScript code between open/close script tags.

HTML comment: it has <!-- to start and --> to end.

<!--write something to remember later like updates you made or thoughts -->

See example for JavaScript and HTML comments:

```
JavaScript Comment.html - Notepad
File   Edit   Format   View   Help

<!DOCTYPE html>
<html>
<head>
  <title>...</title>
</head>

<body>
<!-- HTML comment is outside script tags -->

<script>
// For single line comment in JavaScript

/* For multiline comment in Javascript */
</script>

</body>
</html>
```

8- JavaScript Alert code:

When the web page opens, a message box will come up, which is one of the JavaScript methods.

Example code:

In lower case write: alert ("write your alert message here") put a single or double strings, your choice.

```
JavaScript Alert code.html - Notepad  —  ▢  ✕

File  Edit  Format  View  Help

<!DOCTYPE html>
<html>
<head>
 <title>...</title>
</head>

<body>

<script>

alert("Write somthing here")

</script>

</body>
</html>
```

Result: after saving your .html file, close it, then right click on it and choose Open with from pull down menu and pick you favorite browser to view the code.

The browser execute the code.

Note: in the future you can just refresh the browser to update the code that you save, you don't have to close the .html file.

Google Chrome Result:

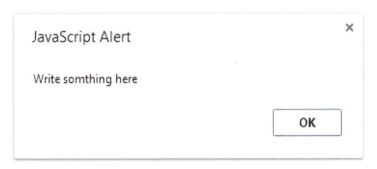

Click **OK** button to close the box.

Mozilla Firefox result:

Internet Explorer result:

Note: if you get a message that Internet explorer restricted the web page from running scripts, Click Allow button.

You can also view the code in **Safari** or **Opera**.

It is a good practice to check the code, spelling, tags and structure to make sure it works.

Note: Size, Font and Icon of the alert box **cannot** be changed unfortunately, **but** you can change the text inside the box.

The good news, JavaScript has much more interesting things to offer than a simple alert box.

9- Summary:

JavaScript is a scripting language and supported by the most popular browser, it is used along with HTML and CSS for the web development.

It uses script open/close tags to tell the user (in this case the web browser) where the scripting language starts and where it ends.

To add a comment in JavaScript we use // for single line comment or /* to start and */ to end the comment which are (/* & */ the same used for multiple line commenting as well.

10- Events Handling:

The execution of the code in JavaScript is as important as the code itself, for example the command *onmouseover* doesn't get done unless the user wants to do so, and move the mouse over something, so there is a time where the code is sitting there and that is what we want it to do just be silent until we decide otherwise, it stays silent until we execute it!

Therefore this is called *event handling,* we have full control, thanks to HTML with JavaScript coding, it allows more page interaction and more control of the events.

JavaScript is an event handler, by clicking anywhere on the page, the interaction.

takes place when the event is detected and the code's execution happens.

Event handlers are mostly attributes, you can use them inside HTML tags and they all start with the "**on**", with **NO space**.

Here are few:

Event	Description
onclick	The user clicks on an element
onmouseover	The user moves the mouse over an element
onchange	When an HTML element is changed
onload	When the page loading is finished
onmouseout	When the mouse moves away from the element
oncontextmenue	When the element is clicked using the right mouse part
ondblclick	When double clicked on the element
onmouseleave	When mouse pointer is out of the element
onmouseup	Mouse button set free over the element

onmousedown	Mouse button held down over the element
onmousemove	Pointer in motion over the element

We add the JavaScript code to the HTML element to allow the event handling attribute.

For that we use "single quotes or double quotes".

Because HTML is not case sensitive so may encounter events that looks something like: onMouseOver or onMOUSEOVER or...That Will not affect anything, but try keeping it lower case such as onmouseover and so on.

<an HTML element   event="JavaScript which is a handler(event)">

Let's see an example:

```
File   Edit   Format   View   Help
<!DOCTYPE html>
<html>
<head>
 <title></title>
</head>
<body>

<p onclick="alert('Have a nice day')">
   Take care!
</p>

</body>
</html>
```

Result:

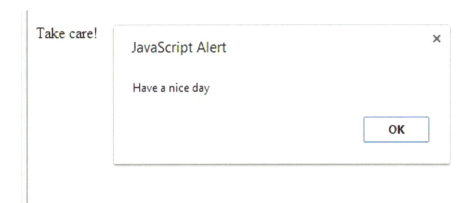

Take care!

At first you will only see the text: Take care!

Click on it and the alert box appear with the message.

Click OK to close the box.

Note: We did Not need to use <script>...</script> tags for the event to happen and be executed, the onclick event handler was good enough, the browser knows that inside the double quotations is the JavaScript code.

11- Nesting:

Nesting is important, you can use either double quotation then single ones Or the inverse start with the single quotations then the double ones, as long as JavaScript is in quotation.

<p onclick="alert('Take care!')"> </p>

OR some they use the single quotations first:

<p onclick='alert("Take care!")'> </p>

The reason of using the first quotation onclick=" Or for some others onclick=' is for the browser to know that it is the start of JavaScript code then " Or ' the closing quotation that it knows it is the end of it.

As long as it has a start quotation matching the end quotation meaning: " and " Or ' and '.

Which is assumed by the browser.

Nesting properly must be otherwise problems executing the event will be encountered.

Something like this example is wrong:

<p onclick="alert('Take care!')"> </p>

Good Practice:

<p onclick=" " Put right away after the onclick= the quotations! Therefore you avoid the mistake.

Remark:

We can use JavaScript code without the script tags, and we can make the execution of events take some time to get executed.

12- <u>The ondblclick:</u>

```
File  Edit  Format  View  Help
<!DOCTYPE html>
<html>
<head>
 <title></title>
</head>
<body>

 <h1 ondblclick="alert('Save a tree')">
  Trees are important
 </h1>


</body>
</html>
```

Result:

In the sentence: Trees are important, each time you double click on a word the message box opens, to close the box click on OK.

You have to double click on a word to trigger the JavaScript code and see the alert box.

13- The onmouseover:

By adding a semi-colon ; you can add more alert messages, by simply moving mouse barely over the h1's text the 1st alert box opens right away, when you close it, the 2nd one appear.

Check the example:

```
File  Edit  Format  View  Help
<!DOCTYPE html>
<html>
<head>
 <title></title>
</head>
<body>

<h1 onmouseover="alert('Save a tree');alert('Help protect the nature')">
 Trees are important
</h1>


</body>
</html>
```

Result: 1st alert box, click OK to close it.

Result: 2nd alert box opens, click OK to close it.

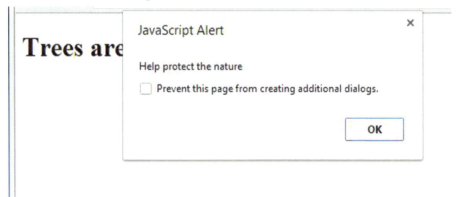

The *prevent* sentence is fine and is from the browser, so has nothing to do with the code.

Note: when using the text editor you save the file, right click on it and use open with, then choose your preferred browser, so it is the same process for viewing the code result.

Once the browser is open you keep saving the updates made to the file and refreshing the browser without having to open it again and again

Click on the arrow to refresh the browser for Google Chrome, Firefox and Internet Explorer but in this one you can as well hit F5.

14- The oncontextmenu:

Check the example:

```
<h1 oncontextmenu="alert('Save a tree')">
  Trees are important
</h1>
```

No code executed once opened in the browser even if you click on the title.

Why? The context menu is a shortcut menu and gets opened with the right click mouse button, for Mac use CTR + Click the subject.

So right click on the title and the alert box opens, click OK, then a menu opens for you with options to choose from, you can just click Esc for escape or click anywhere in the browser to get red of it.

15- Decrease "hot spot":

Let's add an inline style, a border to the h1 text element with the *onclick* event handler.

```
<h1 onclick="alert('Save a tree')" style="border:solid 3px blue">
  Trees are important
</h1>
```

Result: If you click anywhere inside the blue border the alert box opens, the border took the browser width.

To fix that and get only the text to be applied to the event handler not the right empty space you can use span that is as wide as what it contains. Take off the CSS inline style.

The span tag now holds the JavaScript code.

See example:

```
<h1>
<span onclick="alert('Save a tree')">
 Trees are important
</span>
</h1>
```

Result: If you click on the right side of the text nothing will happen, the span now is hot and holds the JavaScript code, and the onclick event handler works just on what the span tag holds within it.

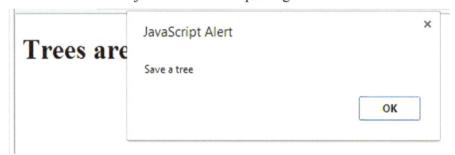

It is good to have control over the JavaScript code.

16- <u>JavaScript Functions:</u>

We used previously the JavaScript <script>...</script> open/close tags in the body section and with event handlers inside HTML tags, and this time we will use it in the head part. So between <head>...</head> open/close tags you can place JavaScript code, which is usually stored in *functions* with name and lines of code. *Functions* organize the code to make it easy to use, to test and debug, can be called from anywhere in the page/pages they give a distinction between HTML and JavaScript code.

JavaScript function is a code that do a particular task, can be called by name.

Example:

Function name( ){

JavaScript code between the curly braces that contains at least one line of coding.

}

You can make up the name, that must start with a letter, after that the use of any symbol or character will be just fine with no spaces. The name has to be easy to remember many people use lower and upper case letters.

<script>...</script> tags placed between <head>...</head> tags contain the functions of the JavaScript code, you can place as many as needed, there is no limit.

Functions as mentioned earlier are used to simplify and organize the code, many lines can be used within the function to fulfill the task, you can call the lines by its simple name and it will be executed easily any time you need to.

Example:

By using text editor, enter the standard HTML5 code which is:

<!DOCTYPE html>

<html>

<head>

<title>...</title>

</head>

<body>

</body>

</html>

Now we can add the <script>...</script> open/close tags to start JavaScript coding in the head part and add the function in between them.

<!DOCTYPE html>

<html>

<head>

<title>...</title>

<script>

function hi(){

....

}

</script>

</head>

<body>...</body>

</html>

The name "hi" is a made up name, you can call your function any name you want to remember it easily later, the function is a JavaScript code because it is included between the <script>...</script> tags and starts with the word function.

the parentheses() are required syntax, can contain parameters inside them must start with a letter without space.

The function above is an empty one and does nothing because nothing was entered between the open/close curly braces "{}", the braces hold the code that the function executes when called.

Very simple example code:

File   Edit   Format   View   Help

```
<!DOCTYPE html>
<html>
<head>
 <title>...</title>

 <script>
  function hi(){
   alert("hi is the name of the Javascript function");
   }
 </script>

</head>
<body>
</body>
</html>
```

The use of the semicolon is not a must but advised and good to have, it acts as a line break that ends the line of code in JavaScript.

Save the file code as ".html or .htm" in your folder and name it "function" or something to remember it later, right click on it to open it, choose Open with, i am using Google Chrome, when the browser you've chosen opens it is blank, because with functions you need to call them to get them execute what you want, and we didn't call the function yet.

Now using the same file you saved earlier, open it and add to it the "input" tag.

```
File   Edit   Format   View   Help
<!DOCTYPE html>
<html>
<head>
 <title>...</title>

 <script>
  function hi(){
   alert("hi is the name of the Javascript function");
  }
 </script>

</head>
<body>
 <input type="button" value="click here" onclick="hi()" />
</body>
</html>
```

Note: "input" tag added in the body section.

Result:

We have a clickable button that onclick executes the function "hi()" placed in the head of HTML5 code.

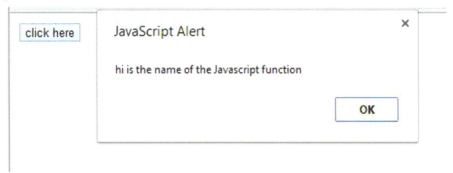

Once you click on "click here" button that appears because of the HTML "input" tag, the alert box opens. Click OK to close it.

The type and value are the attributes of the input tag and both make the button look like one while the event handler "onclick" has the name of the function assigned to it.

Note:

JavaScript is case sensitive.

The tag "input" is just a tag that creates an element and it closes itself.

The event handler "onclick" can be used in any tag that creates a visible element.

To execute the function and call it we just put its name in the event handler.

17- Summary:

We can control what JavaScript does by controlling when to execute the function code.

The <script>...</script> ope/close tags placed in the body part of HTML executes first when opening the browser.

Functions are used to organize the JavaScript code and are placed between <script>...</script> tags in the head section above the <body> open tag.

To identify the function we simply use function word followed by your choice of name,

The code to be executed when called is placed between the curly braces.

The event handler is used to call the function or functions if many to be executed.

18- How to Debug JavaScript:

JavaScript is case sensitive, make sure you type carefully otherwise it will be ignored by the browser.

Quotation marks nested wrong can cause a problem.

Use quotation marks after the event handler: event handler="..." or event handler='...'

Inside the double quotation marks use the single ones and inside the single ones use the double quotation marks.

If the browser still does not execute JavaScript code, check if the JavaScript is enabled.

Check this site on how to enable it: http://www.enable-javascript.com/

19- Introduction:

JavaScript code on its own may appear difficult but once you get to understand it you can even give it a twist to fit your need. It has rules to follow to write it.

Understanding how JavaScript treats the web and document is the first step to do, after that it will make more sense to you how JavaScript handles the web and document as a collection of objects that has properties and methods and ways to be used to handle events that occur when interaction of the user with the page is happening.

No need to be intimidated from words like object, properties and others and no need to panic because they are simple syntax that make the programming easy and fun.

An object is for example a table, that has properties such as a color, the same idea applies to the web.

20- The DOM:

(DOM) stands for "Document Object Model" which constitute a set of rules to manipulate things on the web page. JavaScript is an (OOP) language, which stands for "Object-Oriented Programming" and that applies to any other programming language.

The Document word represents a written information that we can print which in our case is simply the web page.

The Model word has many meanings, but in our case it is the 3D or three dimensional representation of something that could be a person or other. You cannot really touch the Model which is a real representation of a real object but the representation consists of names that we use in JavaScript code.

We define objects through names in "*lowercase*" which is a must in

JavaScript which is a case sensitive language.

Let's check the most popular "object names":

Screen (user's screen like the desktop), window (user's agent window once a browser is open), document (the web page), navigator (browser that shows the page) and the location (the address bar: http://...).

21- The properties of DOM:

JavaScript objects have properties in the DOM, such as color, size, type, brand, etc...

And have materials they are made off as well. In JavaScript properties like font background color, color...which we can manipulate though the JavaScript code.

By writing the *object name* followed by a "*dot*" then the *property name*, therefore: *object.property*

We have the (readOly) and the (readWrite) properties.

21a- readOly: read only field, no changes to be made to the value, but the user can highlight it or copy it and such, it allows to "get the value", it stops the user from modifying the field.

21b- readWrite: gives you flexibility to assign a new value to the property, also allows you to "get the property value" and set it as well.

22- More:

"screen.width" and "screen.height" that gives you the width and height of the screen without ability to modify anything.

"navigator.appVersion"and "navigator.platform" for version info and user's operating system, read only.

"document.title" that gives you the page title which you can modify etc...

23- Methods:

It is the action in JavaScript code, things that the browser will do.

Similar to properties "no spacing" and if too long use of the "camelCase" But the difference is that a method is followed by a pair of parentheses.

Samples code:

"document.getElementById(value)" locates the element that you can control, "window.close()" to close the window etc...

Practice: Let's code with JavaScript using few object's properties and methods.

```
File  Edit  Format  View  Help
<!DOCTYPE html>
<html>
<head>
    <title>Object's Properties and Methods Sample coding</title>
</head>
<body>
  <script> document.write(screen.width)</script> pixels.<br>
  <script> document.write(navigator.platform)</script>.<br>
  <script> document.write(window.innerHeight)</script> pixels.<br>
  <script> document.write(document.lastModified)</script>.<br>
  <script> document.write(document.title)</script>.<br>
  <label for="Address">Enter here:</label>
  <input type="text" id="Address">
  <input type="button" value="SUBMIT"
   onclick="alert(document.getElementById('Address').value)" >
  <button onclick = "window.close()">Close this window</button>

</body>
</html>
```

Result: Displays information about your screen, window height and more.

1366 pixels.
Win32.
319 pixels.
01/06/2015 23:25:49.
Object's Properties and Methods Sample coding.
Enter here: [   ] | SUBMIT | | Close this window |

It is just a normal text with the use of <br> tag that stands for break to end the line.

<script> tag is used to tell the browser we are starting JavaScript code and the "document.write()" uses write() method to write the text at a precise place in the page which depends on what has been put inside the parentheses of the method for example writing (document.title) in the write() method gives or returns the title we entered at the head part. The info you get from (screen.width) will not be the same for all users because it depends on the resolution of user's monitor.

Placing the <script> </script> open/close tags that includes in between the

"document.write()" allows to display the info you wanted to know.

When you click on "Enter here:" the cursor goes to the text box, you can type there the info you want, once you click on SUBMIT button the alert box opens with what you typed into the text box.

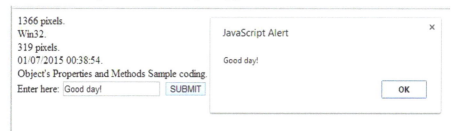

Click OK to close it.

<label>... </label> and <input> tags are HTML tags therefore it is an HTML code.

The part: for="Address" in the label tag which should be equal to the "id" attribute is not required and has no particular thing but when clicking on the text "Enter here:" the cursor moves to the text box which can be called a "control", a "button" is a control that we can click, it is an interaction with the page.

In the <input> tag, the type="text " allows the user to type a text.

Int the <input> tag, the type="button" creates a button with the value or word on it "SUBMIT", onclick="..." is the event handler with the use of *getElementById* method.

The <button> tag displays a button as well, it is a tag for controls same as <input type="button"...> tag, performing the closing window using the *close()* method which works depending on the browser you are using.

24- <u>Literals and Variables:</u>

Don't be intimidated by the title, it is very easy once we get to practice some examples.

Literals are used to represent values that never change, usually enclosed in quotation marks.

Example: *alert("Weather");* an alert box opens in the browser with the text enclosed in the quotation marks, literally means as it is stated, once the code is executed which we saw already, hence is is literal.

```
File   Edit   Format   View   Help
<!DOCTYPE html>
<html>
<head>
    <title></title>
  </head>
<body>
  <script>
  alert("Weather")
  </script>
</body>
</html>
```

Result:

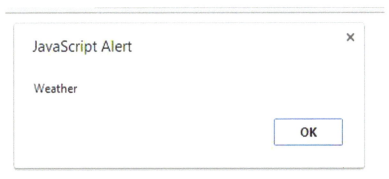

In the *alert("Weather")* Or *alert('Weather')*, the *"Weather"* is *Literal* because it is enclosed in the quotation marks, double or single.

If it was: *alert(Weather), Weather* in this case is a *Variable name.*

Variables are the opposite of the literals, because their values can change. They are containers for storing data values. In Google's home page the text box is available for us to enter something we want to search and find, once we type what we want it stores it and use it to search its database to find the info we are looking for.

The variable syntax in JavaScript is: *var name.*

The name could be anything made-up but unique, the uniqueness of the name is called *identifiers* which can be short names or more specific and descriptive, they follow some rules:

After the first character, the names can have letters, numbers, hyphen or underscores.

Must start with a letter, a dollar sign $, or an _ (underscore).

Are case sensitive, try to make-up the variable names using uppercase and lowercase in a way that makes sense and is easy to remember and recognize.

No empty or blank spaces.

Punctuation authorized are only the hyphen and underscore.

JavaScript Keywords cannot be used as variables or anything else because they are reserved, check the table for a list of some of those reserved words:

arguments	boolean	break	case	catch	default
delete	do	else	enum	export	extends
false	float	for	function	if	import
in	int	long	native	new	null
private	public	return	short	super	switch
this	true	try	typeof	var	void
while	with	yield			

Note: There are more JavaScript reserved words which means words with special meaning than stated in the table.

25- Creating a Variable in JavaScript:

The keyword is *var* then the name of the variable.

Example: *var weather*

In JavaScript, the variable has to be defined so it has to be between <script> </script> open/close tags.

Example:

```
File   Edit   Format   View   Help
<!DOCTYPE html>
<html>
<head>
    <title></title>
  </head>
<body>
   <script>
   var weather
   alert(weather)
   </script>
</body>
</html>
```

Result:

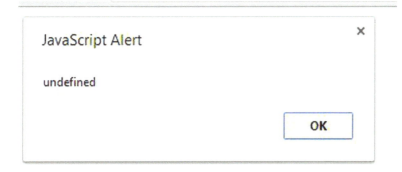

Why do we get *undefined* ?

A variable holds a value, but if the variable doesn't have a value and we didn't give any to *var weather* then its variable's value is undefined.

25a- Value assigned to a variable:

A variable holds an information that might vary which is called a value that is assigned to a variable. The variable name is followed by an = sign where you enter the value.

var name = value is the way to create a variable and assign to it a value.

The = sign is sometimes referred to as an assignment operator.

Example:

```
<body>
  <script>
  var weather = "Cold"
  alert(weather)
  </script>
</body>
```

Result:

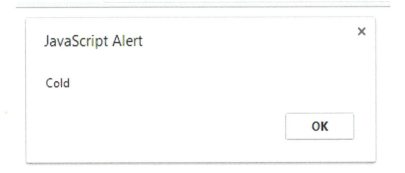

Because we assigned cold as a value to the variable weather, the alert box display cold instead of undefined.

The value assigned can be a number or other. Keep in mind that JavaScript uses variables that holds data or information.

var is used for that purpose, it stores information that later on can be used.

26- Summary:

Like other programming languages JavaScript includes object model and uses variables that holds data or information that might change over time.

DOM, document object model, defines the names used, example screen object defines information of the users screen.

Different objects have different properties, such as color, size etc...

Methods are what the object can do.

Ability to store information using variables.

27- <u>Making Decisions, Numbers and Dates:</u>

27a- <u>Introduction:</u>

What separates JavaScript and other programming languages from a Markup Languages such as HTML, and CSS (style sheet) is the capacity of making decisions that are necessary to make more advanced web pages using functions that make decisions, such as *if...*do this, *else...* do that, etc...

28- <u>Data Types, understanding them:</u>

We have texts data, numbers and dates, as human we know the difference right away but computers need a way to understand that difference because they don't have our intuition.

28a- <u>Strings:</u> are texts.

The Text is used most of the time in programming languages, without a specific numeric value and is held between the quotation marks (double or single), with no specific length and containing any

characters.

Examples:

var name="Nancy"

var email="Nancy1@hotmail.com"

var address="980 bridge park"

The variables (name, email, address) were assigned a string each, which is a text enclosed in quotation marks, in a string we can store anything with the arithmetic being an exception.

28b- <u>Numbers:</u>

Considered quantities (scalar values), include arithmetic such as addition, subtraction, multiplication and such.

Requirements:

- Digits from 0 to 9, one decimal point. Commas, dollar signs, spaces are NOT allowed.

- No quotation marks.

- hyphen is used in front of a number if negative.

Examples:

Allowed:

0	1	-5	1.9	3333.6789

Not allowed:

155-66-3	H1B 7A5	(345)66-111	234,65	23,11.09	$45.99

Remark: we cannot store phone numbers, social numbers, dollar sign, postal or zip code because they are not really numbers and fulfill specific purposes, can be stored as strings.

Any application of math on any dollar amount should be stored as numbers with No currency sign or commas.

To apply arithmetic we use symbols called *Operators*.

Operator	Operator	Operator	Operator
+ (Addition)	- (Subtraction)	* (Multiplication)	/ (Division)

Usually the math in JavaScript is simple but can be complex when needed.

Example:

Note: we can make-up names if we wish to and as many as we like.

var numb = 9

Therefore creation of a variable named *numb* (a shortcut for number), set to equal 9, no quotation marks as it is an arithmetic variable and no strings to be used in this case.

var price = 3.99

The variable *var price* stores the price as being equal to 3.99.

*var total = numb * price*

The *var total* variable stores the total which is the number 9 multiplied by the price 3.99 values using the operator * (multiplication).

Note: any text between // and the end of the line will not be executed as it is just a comment in JavaScript, so it will be ignored.

// is called single line comments usually used to comment or write notes to explain what it is about.

Let's use the *.write* method: document.write(total) to display the result.

To avoid the the 2 results from being side by side we use the document.write() and add to it the tag <br> so that the JavaScript result appear on one line and the fixed one to 3 decimal places below.

document.write(total.toFixed(3)) is used to set the decimal part to just 3 numbers (check the result of the 2nd line)

JavaScript js

File   Edit   Format   View   Help

```
<!DOCTYPE html>
<html>
<head>
<title>Sample Numbers</title>
</head>
<body>
  <script>
    //variable named numb stores a number 9
    var numb = 9
    //variable named price stores a number 3.99
    var price = 3.99
    //variable named total multiply the numbers 9 and 3.99
    var total = numb * price
    //to display the var total result
    document.write(total)
    //the use of the break tag to display results in 2 lines
    document.write("<br>")
    //multiplication result with just 3 decimal places
    document.write(total.toFixed(3))
  </script>
</body>
</html>
```

Result:

35.910000000000004
35.910

28c- Dates:

In JavaScript we can use and store dates, by calculating the past days and the future one or days in between two dates, for this to work we must store it as a date object.

The syntax to do this is different than the ones used for strings and numbers.

40

var name = new date ( )

By using commas we can store separate values such as:

var name = new Date (year, month)

You can replace year with 4 digits and the month with a number from 0 to11 because the list in JavaScript language always starts with 0 not 1 which makes sense when doing the math and making the code run faster.

Another way to store dates is by using a string (single or double quotation marks).

Example: var name = new Date ("November 16 2012")

It is possible to add a time to the date, just after the year with a space using:

hours:minutes:seconds

Example: var name = new Date ("November 16 2012 14:25:00")

14:25:00 stands for 2:25 PM.

Sample:

```
File  Edit  Format  View  Help
<!DOCTYPE html>
<html>
<head>
<title>Ways to store Dates</title>
</head>
<body>
  <script>
    //variable named birthday
    var birthday = new Date()
    //store dates and times
    var birthday = new Date(1975,1,16)
    var vacation = new Date("November 28 2012")
    var vacations = new Date("December 21 2013 14:45:00")
    //Display results and use of the <br> tag to place them on # lines
    document.write(birthday)
    document.write("<br>")
    document.write(vacation)
    document.write("<br>")
    document.write(vacations)
  </script>
</body>
</html>
```

Result: values, stored as dates in a specific format.

Sun Feb 16 1975 00:00:00 GMT-0700 (Mountain Standard Time)
Wed Nov 28 2012 00:00:00 GMT-0700 (Mountain Standard Time)
Sat Dec 21 2013 14:45:00 GMT-0700 (Mountain Standard Time)

If no time was specified, it shows as midnight which is 00:00:00.

GMT stands for Greenwich Mean Time and is a standard, the number after that is the number of hours different than the GMT.

28d- Boolean data type:

Very simple data type that has one of the two values, true or false, if we assign another value other than the previous two, it will return false or true.

Often we need a data type similar to: YES / NO, ON / OFF, TRUE /

FALSE which applies to the Boolean data type, real values are true, and non real ones are false.

0, -0, "", null, NaN (means Not-a-Number), undefined (no value assigned to the variable name), all these will return false but assigning any other values will return true.

Note: no quotation marks for the Boolean value.

You can set the value to false or true.

Sample:

```
File  Edit  Format  View  Help
<!DOCTYPE html>
<html>
<head>
<title>Boolean</title>
</head>
<body>
  <script>
    //variable named true
    var name1 = true
    //variable named false
    var name2 = false
    //Display results and use of the <br> tag to place them on # lines
    document.write(name1)
    document.write("<br>")
    document.write(name2)
  </script>
</body>
</html>
```

Result:

```
true
false
```

Boolean term came from George Boole, an English mathematician whose algebraic logic is based on 0 and 1which all modern computing is based on.

Boolean variables are simple but useful, with using if...then...else decisions and based on Boolean values there are things happening behind the scenes that we don't see.

29- Decision Making:

The steps in writing simple decision making code is by using the " *if* " statement same as human making decisions but in a language the computer understands.

29a- " if " Statements:

If is a condition for the code to be executed, it is the name of a Boolean variable which has true or false result, if and only if the condition is true the code is executed, otherwise it will be ignored.

Rules:

- *if* must be lower case letters.

- The condition must be placed inside parentheses such as : *if (condition)*.

Sample:

Note: // is just a comment in JavaScript.

```
File  Edit  Format  View  Help
<!DOCTYPE html>
<html>
<head>
   <title>if (one line statement)</title>
</head>
<body>
<script>
   var condition = true;
   if (condition) document.write("condition is true");
</script>
</body>
</html>
```

Result in the browser:

condition is true

The variable named *condition* has true as value, *document.write("condition is true")* once executed displays the sentence between the parentheses.

Now let's set the value of the variable to *false*.

Sample:

```
<body>
<script>
    var condition = false;
    if (condition) document.write("condition is true");
</script>
</body>
```

Result: Web page is Blank! Why? Because the code that writes *condition is true* is only executed when the variable named *condition* has true as value, if it has false instead it will be ignored and the web page therefore is blank.

29b- " if " statements, multiple code lines:

For multilines if statement to be execute when a condition is true we will use a pair of curly braces to enclose the JavaScript codes.

If (condition) {

   Code to execute if the condition is true;

   Type another code...;

   And so on ...keep typing your codes...;

}

The curly braces enclose the block of code to be executed if the condition is true and to be ignored if the condition is false.

29c- "else" option added:

In this way we can use a block of codes that will be executed if the condition is false.

By adding the *else* word and a pair of *curly braces.*

if (condition) {

 block of code to be executed;

} else {

 block of code to be executed;

}

if is in lowercase, the condition is enclosed in the parentheses and the curly braces enclose the code to be executed.

It is a good practice to always type the parentheses and curly braces at first then fill them to avoid forgetting them.

Sample:

```
File  Edit  Format  View  Help
<!DOCTYPE html>
<html>
<head>
    <title>if else statment</title>
</head>
<body>
<script>
  var condition = false;
  if (condition) {
    document.write("condition is true");
  } else {
    document.write("condition is false");
  }
</script>
</body>
</html>
```

Result:

condition is false

The Boolean variable of the condition is set to false, therefore it displays *condition is false.*

Let's change the value of the variable named condition to true instead.

Sample code:

```
<script>
  var condition = true;
  if (condition) {
    document.write("condition is true");
  } else {
    document.write("condition is false");
  }
</script>
```

Result:

condition is true

29d- Other *if* statements:

Multiple conditions:

Nesting if statements for different conditions gives different actions.

Sample:

if (conditionA) {

block of code to execute if conditionA is true

} else if (conditionB) {

    block of code to execute if conditionB is true

} else {

    block of code to execute if conditionA is false and conditionB is false

}

Before the final *else* we can use many conditions and between any pair of braces we can have many lines of code to be executed.

30- Conditions, explained:

The *if* statement is about having the code make decisions regarding steps to do, it is conditional and found in all programming languages, the condition is a test to see if a certain condition is true or false involving comparisons.

Applying these tests need expressions that use operators.

Example: grade > 80 means the variable *grade* contains a number, if it is greater than 80 it returns true and if the grade is less than 80 then the condition is false therefore it returns false.

There are many comparison operators to write expressions.

30a- Operators:

Operator	Means	Example
==	equal to	x==5
>	grater than	x>5
<	less than	x<5
>=	greater than or equal to	x>=5
<=	less than or equal to	x<=5
!=	not equal	x!=5

Note: == means equal, not to get confused with the one = sign which is the assignment operator used to store a value in a variable.

Sample:

var x = 5

We created a variable named x and assigned to it the value 5, there is no comparison at all. We stored the number 5 in the variable named x. Let's check the table in this case.

Example	Returns
x==5	true
x>5	false
x<5	false
x>=5	true
x<=5	true
x!=5	false

Sample code:

```
File  Edit  Format  View  Help
<!DOCTYPE html>
<html>
<head>
   <title>if else statment</title>
</head>
<body>
<script>
  var score = 80;
  if (score >= 73) {
     document.write("The score is high");
  } else {
     document.write("The score is low");
  }
</script>
</body>
</html>
```

Result:

The score is high

The if code executes because the condition *score >= 73* is true, therefore the web displays *The score is high.*

Some testing conditions are not simple and need other type of operators called the Logical Operators.

30b- Logical Operators:

JavaScript Logical Operators are used to establish the logic between variables or values they allow testing for many conditions to determine if all or some of them are true or not.

Let's consider two variable, x = 5 and y = 9.

Operator	Means	Example
&&	and	(x < 7 && y > 4) is true
!	not	!(x == y) is true
||	or	(x == 3 || y == 3) is false

More complex sample:

Which is actually very simple if we look at each step.

```
<body>
<script>
    var age = 90
    if (age <= 13) {
        document.write("cannot drive")
    }
    else if (age > 16 && age < 85) {
        document.write("can drive")
    } else {
        document.write("someone else should drive")
    }
</script>
</body>
```

Result:

someone else should drive

Explanation:

var age = 90 (creates a variable named age and stores 90 as value).

if (age <= 13) {

  document.write("cannot drive")

}

That means if age is less than or equal to 13 the person *cannot drive* and since 90 is over that it will not happen.

else if (age > 16 && age < 85) {

document.write("can drive")

}

That means if age is greater than 16 and less than 85 the person *can drive* but it is not the case as the var age is set to 90.

else {

document.write("someone else should drive")

}

Therefore the *else* statement will be executed and the web displays *someone else should drive.*

31- Summary:

JavaScript language stores data to create interactive web pages.

- Boolean values are either true or false.

- Dates are such as month, day, year or simply time.

- Numbers are scalar values

- Strings are texts such as names.

The *if...else* logic allows the code to make decisions based on the variable's values which helps developing websites and more.

32- Searching the site:

Let' get started with the usual HTML controls and HTML5 tags and coding to allow word searching.

Open the editor in my case Notepad, or any of your choice and start coding.

Sample:

```
File  Edit  Format  View  Help
<!DOCTYPE html>
<html>
<head>
<title>Searching the web</title>
</head>
<body>
 <script>
  <p>Searching the web
    <input type="text" id="wordtofind" autofocus>
    <input type="button" onclick="search()" value="find"
  </p>
 </script>
</body>
</html>
```

When you save it as .html or .htm then open it in the browser nothing shows-up, why?

Because we need JavaScript code to make the search happen and take place.

So below the </title> closing tag but above the </head> closing tag, we need to add the <script> opening tag then close it by adding the </script> closing tag.

```
<head>
<title>Searching the web</title>
<script>
</script>
</head>
```

The use of the *onclick="search()"* in the input tag, is for the code to find the function search() once the button is clicked.

```
<head>
<title>Searching the web</title>
<script>
  function search () {
  }
</script>
</head>
```

Notice that now we have a JavaScript function *search ( )* but still it does nothing because it is empty. The code to be executed is enclosed between the opening and closing curly braces.

When calling the function write the website name you need to find, get what the user typed, create a URL (Uniform Resource Locator: http://...) and put it in the address bar, if the text box wasn't filled at all and still empty then use alert to remind the user to type something.

You can use any site's name that you know to began searching, if you have your own site then you can use it instead.

Start coding between the open/close curly braces, you can use comments to make notes to yourself as a reminder if you wish by using //...*type here what you want.*

```
<script>
  function search () {
    //use any website's name you want
    var site = "dictionary.cambridge.org";
  }
</script>
```

To get what the user typed in the text box we use *document.getElementById,* in our sample the id in the input tag was *id="wordtofind"* we can get its value which in JavaScript means whatever the user typed. Let's add this to our code.

```
<head>
<title>Searching the web</title>
<script>
  function search () {
    //use any website's name you want
    var site = "dictionary.cambridge.org";
    //the text that the user typed
    var find = "document.getElementById("wordtofind") .value;
  }
</script>
</head>
```

A variable named *find* was added, it will store the data that the user typed in the text box.

32a- <u>Searching:</u>

If the user typed the text in the text box the code will perform the search but in case left blank then the user gets an alert message to type something.

Sample: same as before but adding the *if & else* block.

```
<head>
<title>Searching the web</title>
<script>
  function search () {
    //use any website's name you want
    var site = "dictionary.cambridge.org";
    //the text that the user typed
    var find = "document.getElementById("wordtofind") .value;
    //Adding the if...else block, case: textbox not empty
    if () {
    } else {
    }

  }
</script>
</head>
```

Note: the last closing curly brace closes the whole block of code, it belongs to the code

function search ( ) {

    block of code to be executed

}

The use of *if* is to make a decision based on the text box being blank or not. We have a variable named ***find*** therefore anything stored in that text box is that variable which is a string type because it is in the text box.

32b- .length property:

Use the syntax: string.length

If you wish to find the length of the string typed by the user the *.length* property allows you to do that, it determines the number of characters, if the text box was blank then the the result will show 0 (the number zero).

Sample:

```
File  Edit  Format  View  Help
<!DOCTYPE html>
<html>
<head>
</head>

<body>
<p>The length of a string in JavaScript.</p>
<button onclick="myfunction()">Click here</button>
<p id="test"></p>

<script>
 function myfunction() {
    var string = "Hi there";
    var number = string.length;
    document.getElementById("test").innerHTML = number;
}
</script>
</body>
</html>
```

Result:

The length of a string in JavaScript.

Click here

8

Note: the space is also a character that why we have 8 for the string "Hi there".

The code sends a URL (Uniform Resource Locator) which is an address to Google when performing the search, therefore Google search for it and finds it, we can also enter a site name in the search text box.

The *string concatenation* in the programming language builds the URL, to join two or more strings.

33- String concatenation:

A string is a text, concatenation means "linking or joining things together" like a chain, so let's say we have two strings *Hi* and *There*, if we concatenate them together we get *Hi There,* it is that simple.

To concatenate simply use JavaScript + operator.

In the case of strings (not numbers) the + operator joins two or more strings to make a single one, example: "Hi" + "There" gets us one single string which is "Hi There".

Sample:

```
<body>
<p>Click on the button to join strings</p>
<button onclick="myfunction()">Click here</button>
<p id="test"></p>

<script>
 function myfunction() {
   var string1 = "Hi ";
   var string2 = "There!";
   var string3 = " How are you?";
   var result = string1.concat(string2,string3);
   document.getElementById("test").innerHTML = result;
}
</script>
</body>
```

Result:

Click on the button to join strings

Click here

Hi There! How are you?

Once you click the button the sentence below appears.

String concat() method is very simple, it returns a new string of the joined strings without changing the existing ones.

34- Drop Down List:

Adding a drop-down list that holds selections and choices for the user is helpful, by using HTML controls and JavaScript coding.

Many websites have a drop-down lists, the controls are just a text box with an arrow on its side, by clicking on the arrow the selection list shows up.

To add a drop-down menu or list we use HTML opening and closing tags:

<select>...</select> and <option>...</option>.

By adding an *id* to <select> tag or element you allow the selection from the list through JavaScript, an ID name is needed for the control because JavaScript finds controls only through ID's.

The <option> tag inside the <select> element which is itself a control that enables to collect user data states the convenient options in the list.

In each option you can use a value that has a unique item, JavaScript determines the value or which choice the user picked through the value of the item chosen.

To end the control use </select> closing tag.

Sample:

Note: <!-- write your comment here --> is the HTML comment tag.

* * is an HTML entity used for non-breaking space.

```
<body>
 <p>Search here:
    <input type="text" id="texttofind" autofocus>
    <!-- search textbox and text -->
     Pick:
    <input type="button" onclick="search()" value="Click">
 </p>
</body>
```

Result: Text box created followed by a text and a button on the same line.

To show the drop-down list we add the <select> control as mentioned earlier that needs an ID for the JavaScript to get the selected item, the ID is a made-up name and is case sensitive with no spaces and must start with a letter.

```
<body>
 <p>Search here:
    <input type="text" id="texttofind" autofocus>
    <!-- search textbox and text -->
     Pick:
    <select id="dropdownlist">

    </select>
    <input type="button" onclick="search()" value="Click">
 </p>
</body>
```

Result:

| Search here: | | Pick: | ⌄ | Click |

Now let's add the <option> </option> open/close tags to state the items to select from in the drop-down list, we will also add a unique value that has an attribute with or without a number to each option to allow JavaScript to make decisions regarding the steps to take based on the user's choice.

The <option> </option> open/close tags with the values are added between the

<select> </select> open/close tags.

Sample:

```
<body>
  <p>Search here:
    <input type="text" id="texttofind" autofocus>
    <!-- Drop down list -->
     Pick:
    <select id="dropdownlist">
      <option value="blue">Blue</option>
      <option value="yellow">Yellow</option>
      <option value="green">Green</option>
      <option value="red">Red</option>
    </select>
    <input type="button" onclick="search()" value="Click">
  </p>
</body>
```

Result:

| Search here: | | Pick: | Blue ⌄ | Click |

Click the arrow:

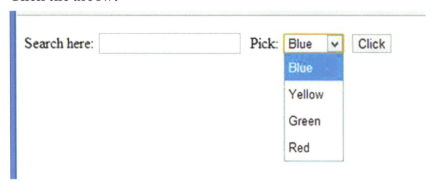

The selection or drop down list is added, the user can choose by clicking on the arrow then selecting any value he needs.

34a- The Default Selection and changing it:

Note: *Blue* shows up first in the selection box because it was the first item in the list.

So *Blue* is the default selection in this case, but you can bring to the top any item you want to show first and all what you need to do is put it in the first <option>...</option>

tags when coding.

The order of the items is not required but may be used such as numbers starting from the smallest to the largest and the alphabetical order for expressions.

Note: There is another way to select a default without rearranging items.

Let's make *Yellow* a default search in the drop down box without changing the order of items.

Sample:

```
<option value="yellow" selected>Yellow</option>
```

Result:

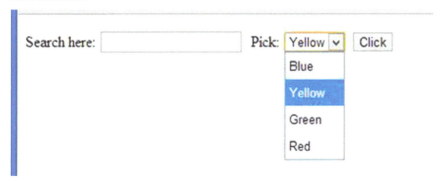

As you can see by just adding *selected* with a space after the value "yellow" and before the <mark>></mark> of the option tag, the *Yellow* become the top item in the selection list, of course Blue still in the list but not anymore as a default.

35- Summary:

- String concatenation is used to join two or more strings to just one single string by using

  JavaScript + operator.

- Showing a drop down list by using HTML <select> and <option> tags.

- Use of *selected* in <option> tag allows to choose a default item from the drop down list.

36- Introduction:

HTML uses <audio> and <video> tags for sounds and videos, no need for plug-ins with possible variety of sound and media players.

But JavaScript gives more control, more freedom to use these elements and instead of just displaying them it adds background and sound effects which are necessary and fun.

If you have few sounds and media files feel free to use them, otherwise you can download free ones from internet for learning purpose.

37- <u>Sound:</u>

There are many formats for the sound, the file name's extension is its format .

examples:

MP3, MP4, WAV etc... The difference between them is about the way the sound file is compressed without the lost of the quality, most public domain methods and techniques are not patented, for example MP3 which is supported by most browsers.

On the other hand if the format is not patented and is free to use, the song or product is a protected copyright meaning no distribution allowed, fortunately some are *public domain* and free to be used.

Let's start coding with HTML5 and use its required tags:

<!DOCTYPE html>

<html>

<head>

<title></title>

</head>

<body>

</body>

</html>

Use Notepad or one of your choice text editor and save the HTML5 code file as sound.html or sound.htm.

Note:

Check first if your browser handles the HTML5 audio, the syntax to use for object detection is simple:

if (window.HTMLAudioElement) {

    Write your code here....

}

If any code between the curly braces is executed, the browser supports the HTML5 audio, otherwise it doesn't.

38- Player creation:

To control the sound through JavaScript, we need an HTML5 object video, an invisible one, so instead of viewing we just control the sound and the syntax or code to use is:

```
<script>
  if (window.HTMLAudioElement) {
      Var player = document.createElement("sound")
}
```

That means creating an HTML5 sound player if the HTML5 audio is supported, if not supported the code will be simply ignored.

Property: " .canPlayType "

After defining an audio player use *.canPlayType* property, this method checks the ability of the browser to play the audio/video type and can return either probably, maybe or an empty string """, it is an unusual property because it returns a string instead of true or false. An empty string """ (zero) tells us right away that it cannot play the file.

Using the .canPlayType ('mimetype'):

To test for more than one type we use *.canPlayType ('mimetype').*

MIME means: Multipurpose Internet Mail Extensions that allows exchange of data files such as audio and video on the internet.

A mime type is a string that has two parts, a type and a subtype

MP3 is supported by most browsers, the type and subtype of the file extension .mp3 for example are: audio/mpeg3, audio/x-mpeg-3, video/mpeg and video/x-mpeg, where x means non-standard.

To use this code give a name to your player and replace *mimetype* with the file type, such as: *name.canPlayType('mimetype')*.

MP3: simple *audio/mpeg* format.

OGG: complex, codecs (compressor/decompressor).

39- Compatibility Check:

In JavaScript we check the compatibility by using the *if* block code.

Let's test for MP3:

if (name.canPlayType ('audio/mpeg').length > 0) {

*   block code...*

}

Replace the *name* with the audio object's name which is the player's name, then between the curly braces write your code to set the audio's appropriate sound file.

Keep in mind, the browser need to support the HTML5 audio, if yes then state a player to play the audio and find out if the browser plays MP3.

40- Method: *setAttribute( )*

We need the *setAttribute( )* which is a JavaScript method to set the HTML's element attribute.

Attributes are inside HTML tags they give us specific information regarding the HTML element, we use *name="value"* for that.

Examples of tags or elements with attributes in HTML code:

41- The HTML <a> anchor tag:

To create a link we use the <a> tag followed by its attribute *href* which specifies the link's destination and without it the <a> tag is not a hyperlink.

Sample code:

<a href="http://www.wikipedia.org" target="_blank">wikipedia</a>

Note:

http://www.wikipedia.org is the value assigned to the *href* attribute.

target="_blank" opens the link in a new window.

target is also an attribute that has *_blank* as a value.

42- The HTML <img> tag:

Used to insert an image.

Sample code:

<img src="girl.png" alt="picture">

src is an attribute, *girl.png* is the value assigned to src and is just a picture I saved and gave it a file name *girl.png.*

alt is an attribute as well with *picture*.

43- Property: *setAttribute*

The *setAttribute* method allow setting the value of the attribute in JavaScript.

Code:

element.setAttribute(attributename, value)

element: is a variable for a defined element that is identified with getElementById( ) and for which we set and modify the attribute.

attributename: such as *src* for <img> tag, it is the attribute that we assign a value to.

value: is assigned to the attribute.

The *setAttribute* property is helpful.

<audio> element defines sound content, MP3, OGG and Wav are 3 supported format files. HTML5 is a standard to play audio files in a web page, many browsers support it but if it doesn't a file conversion online is available, such as the use of *media.io* website to do so.

Sample:

To do this just save an MP3 or OGG sound file to your computer in the same folder where you saved the code file otherwise it will not work, then open it with your preferred browser, src stands for the source that equals the sound file name previously saved.

eat.mp3 sound file is used   in the sample code.

```
<audio src="eat.mp3" controls>
</audio>
```

OR:

```
<audio controls>
    <source src="eat.mp3">
</audio>
```

Result:

Few attributes for the <audio> tag include:

src: its value is just an URL of the audio file.

autoplay: with this attribute the audio begins to play.

controls: if included the audio file will have controls which is nice to have and its value is just "controls".

loop: once the audio finishes it starts again.

preload: it has three parameters, auto, metadata and none.

Note: to make the file work in all browsers we just use *<source>* element.

Sample:

```
<audio controls>
    <source src="eat.mp3">
</audio>
```

44- JavaScript Audio:

<audio src="soundfile" controls>

</audio>

The *soundfile* will be replaced with the audio file of your choice, the *src* is an attribute for setting a value, setAttribute can be used in JavaScript to tell it which sound file to play.

45- Sound Effects:

In response to an event the sound plays, such as by clicking a button.

Let's create a button and write the function code that when the button is clicked it calls that JavaScript function.

<button onclick="play( )">Try</button>

function play( ) {

if (window.player) {

player.play( ); }

}

When we call the *function play( )* the event is executed, in this code sample, when the button is clicked, the object named *player* is searched for, therefore the reason for using the *if (window.player)*.

If the object is found the result is *true,* the *.play( )* method gets HTML5 to play the audio player which is then executed, but if not found it returns *false.*

Note:

The latest version of HTML called HTML5 possess controls that were not available before. A browser playing HTML5 audio doesn't mean its ability to display range controls.

The *window.HTMLAudioElement* allow access to the <audio> methods and elements properties for manipulation.

The *if(window.HTMLAudioElement)* is used to test if the browser handles the HTML5 audio with input controls.

46- Applying CSS:

CSS is used for styling websites and can be controlled using JavaScript which has ability to make decisions in an intelligent way, but the name of the property used in JavaScript and CSS is not always the same which is unfortunate, in JavaScript we need to eliminate the hyphen and capitalize the first letter after it.

Table of some properties:

CSS Properties	Description	JavaScript properties
background	Specifies the background properties	background
background-color	Specifies the background color	backgroundColor
background-image	Specifies the background image	backgroundImage
background-size	Specifies the size of the background	backgroundSize
border-color	Specifies the color of the border	borderColor
color	Specifies the color of the text	color
font-family	Specifies the font family of the text	fontFamily
font-size	Specifies the font size of the text	fontSize
text-align	Specifies the horizontal alignment of the text	textAlign

47- Summary:

HTML5 audio doesn't need plug-ins in order to play.

<audio> </audio> tags allow the audio object to be controlled by using JavaScript.

Possible creation of audio object in a browser that supports it.

.canPlayType( ), .play( ) and .pause( ) methods allow the control of when and what the player plays.

.setAttribute allows a value assignment to any HTML tag.

.style property allows CSS to be applied to elements through JavaScript.

48- Arrays and Loops:

48a- Creating Arrays:

Sometimes in programming you need to work with lists of items and the best way to do it is by having a group of file names in a list, therefore it is easier to work with them through their positions in the list which can be expressed in numbers which computers are known to be great at comprehending.

The list of items is visible to the programming language not people and through the programming language it can be accessed and manipulated, we refer to this type of list as an *array* to differentiate it from the visible lists on a page.

1) JavaScript Array:

The array object in JavaScript has properties and methods to help work with data which is stored in arrays that are just lists in the computer memory.

An array is a variable that is capable of holding more than one value at once.

Code:

var name = new Array( )

Where *name* will be replaced by your chosen variable name that must start with a letter with no spaces or symbols. The code tells JavaScript the intention of creating an array.

In *Array( )* we used uppercase A which is typical in JavaScript's object name.

We need the assignment operator =, all items have the same name and to differentiate between them we just give each a number in square brackets.

The number starts from 0 and so on...not from 1, so [0] is the first element in the array and [1] is the second one.

We can have different types of variables in the same array, we can have names, numbers, objects, functions, arrays within the array etc...

Sample for Array coding:

```
File  Edit  Format  View  Help
<!DOCTYPE html>
<html>
<head>
<title>Array coding</title>
</head>
<body>
<p id="test"></p>

<script>
var cars= new Array ("BMW", "Mazda", "Mercedes");
document.getElementById("test").innerHTML = cars[0];
</script>

</body>
</html>
```

Result:

BMW

We can write the same code by replacing the *new Array* by **[ ]** instead.

```
<body>
<p id="test"></p>

<script>
var cars= ["BMW", "Mazda", "Mercedes"];
document.getElementById("test").innerHTML = cars[0];
</script>
</body>
```

Result: same as previous for *cars[0]*.

BMW

Sample code:

var cars= new Array()

car[0] = "BMW";

car[1] = "Mazda";

car[2] = "Mercedes";

Developer use the word *sub* for subscript values, so car[0] is said *car sub zero*.

In the sample we stored a string in each array, which could be names of any kind, human, product or others, the variable name stayed the same for all and instead of changing it we just changed the subscript number, which gives us a huge programming abilities.

The element is the item in the array, it is different than the web elements such as paragraphs etc...

Note: the elements in an array do not appear on the web page, they are just facts kept in memory similar to JavaScript variable.

Sample code: Another way to create arrays is the condensed way.

var cars = new Array("BMW", "Mazda","Mercedes");

By having all the values separated by commas inside the parentheses we save time coding, it is a condensed one code instead of many. We enclosed them in quotation marks (string) because they are texts, subscripts are assigned automatically starting at 0 (zero).

An even shorter code: known as the *array initializer* or *array literal.*

var cars = ["BMW", "Mazda","Mercedes"];

The array elements are put in square brackets and are separated by commas.

Note: in all the different ways to code arrays the end result is the same.

You might prefer the longer code because it is clearer to read or you might go for the shorter one to keep it clean, the choice is yours.

2) Array Properties:

a) .length:

Its value is an integer with a positive sign, you can use this property to truncate an array without increasing the actual elements if you wish to extend.

Creating an array means creating an object in JavaScript which can be tested by using some properties such as *.length* which specifies the number of elements in an array.

Code that returns the array length: *arrayname.length*

In the previous example we had an array named cars that had three elements(car brands)

The code for it would be: *cars.length*

The result would be 3 because we have 3 elements in that array.

Code that sets the array length: *array.length = number*

Sample:

```
<!DOCTYPE html>
 <html>
<head>
    <title></title>
</head>
<body>
<script>
    var cars = ["BMW", "Mazda", "Mercedes"]
    alert(cars.length)
</script>
</body>
</html>
```

Code:

```
File  Edit  Format  View  Help
<!DOCTYPE html>
  <html>
<head>
   <title></title>
</head>
<body>
<script>
   var cars = ["BMW", "Mazda", "Mercedes"]
   alert(cars.length)
</script>
</body>
</html>
```

Result:

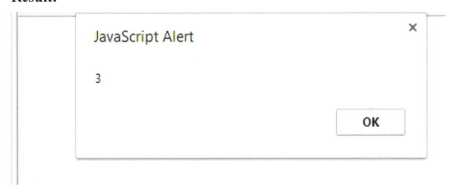

The alert box shows the number 3 as we have 3 elements in the array.

If we had more or less elements in the array then the alert box will reflect the number matching their number.

3) Array Methods:

To manipulate the array elements we use methods, the popular ones are .*sort( )* and .*reverse( )*.

a) .*sort( )* **method:** sorts the items that can be ascending or descending, numeric or alphabetic. When sorting strings (text) it gives an alphabetical order from A to Z (the ascending way) by default, but when sorting numbers as strings for example "32" and "100", "32" is bigger than "100" because "3" is bigger than "1" which is an incorrect result, and to fix that you need to change the original array by calling

76

the compare function.

Samples:

```
<body>
<p>Click to sort the order of the elements in the array.</p>

<button onclick="myFunction()">Click me</button>

<p id="test"></p>

<script>
   var cars = ["Mazda", "BMW", "Mercedes"]
   document.getElementById("test").innerHTML = cars;

   function myFunction() {
   cars.sort();
   document.getElementById("test").innerHTML = cars;
}
</script>
</body>
```

Result: Once the button is clicked the elements get sorted in an ascending alphabetical way.

Click to sort the order of the elements in the array.

Click me

BMW,Mazda,Mercedes

b) *.reverse( )* **method:** reverses the order of the elements from their previous one, so if the .sort( ) was used .reverse( ) method puts the elements in a descending order.

Sample:

```
<body>

<p>Click to reverse the order of the elements in the array.</p>
<button onclick="myFunction()">Click me</button>
<p id="test"></p>

<script>
    var cars = ["BMW", "Mazda", "Mercedes"]
    document.getElementById("test").innerHTML = cars;

    function myFunction() {
    cars.reverse();
    document.getElementById("test").innerHTML = cars;
}
</script>
</body>
```

Result: Once the button is clicked the elements get a descending alphabetical order.

Click to reverse the order of the elements in the array.

Click me

Mercedes,Mazda,BMW

You can combine the codes for .*sort( )* and .*reverse( )* together to end up with the same results, while by default the first method organize the elements inside the array in an ascending way, the second one reverse that order.

Arrays can be used in a creative way to make cool things in apps and websites but the coolest of all is the *looping trough* the array.

c) .join( ) Method:

The Array's elements are joined into a string.

Sample:

```
<body>

<p>Join the array elements into a string.</p>
<button onclick="myFunction()">Click me</button>
<p id="test"></p>

<script>
   function myFunction() {
   var cars = ["BMW", "Mazda", "Mercedes"];
   var z = document.getElementById("test");
   z.innerHTML = cars.join();
}
</script>
</body>
```

The code can be simpler by not adding the *var z* or any other variable name, it work just fine without it, the .join( ) method is for demonstration purpose, therefore a var name is added.

```
<script>
   function myFunction() {
   var cars = ["BMW", "Mazda", "Mercedes"]
   document.getElementById("test").innerHTML = cars;
}
</script>
```

Result:

Join the array elements into a string.

Click me

BMW,Mazda,Mercedes

Another sample for .join( ) Method:

```
<script>
    function myFunction() {
    var cars = ["BMW", "Mazda", "Mercedes"];
    var z = document.getElementById("test");
    z.innerHTML = cars.join(" or ");
}
</script>
```

Result:

Join the array elements into a string.

Click me

BMW or Mazda or Mercedes

48b- Loops:

Like many programming languages JavaScript has *loops* which consist of a block of code repeated many times until it reaches a specific condition. It helps saving time and avoiding rewriting the same code over and over again, they are used to access elements in an array, there are two types of loops.

1) JavaScript *for* loop:

It is used to create a loop and supply a means of its repetition at an established number of times at the same time of incrementing or decrementing the value of some variable, so it offers the possibility to count forward or backward, also to start and end at any number.

We use the *for* statement as a counter, we need the starting point which is the initial value of the counting start, the condition to test to determine the continuation of the loop and if it is true the increment or decrement to be executed, after the complete execution the loop restarts again.

for (start, condition, increment or decrement) {

   code to be executed

}

Note: All the parts of the *for loop* occur at the same time.

- The *i* is the label for the counter variable which is used to count how many times the *for loop* has looped.

- The *condition* to decide whether or not the *for loop* continues the execution and usually includes the counter variable.

- After each loop the counter variable is incremented or decremented.

Then comes the code to be executed for each loop.

Sample:

for (start, condition, increment or decrement) {

   code to be executed

}

For *start* part let's replace it by a variable named *i* and assign an initial value to it.

For *condition* part let's set when the loop stops repeating.

For *increment* part let's set the amount of increments or decrements, we can use ++ to increment or -- to decrement the value by 1.

Finally the code to be executed each time.

```
File  Edit  Format  View  Help
<!DOCTYPE html>
<html>
<head>
<title>the for loop</title>
</head>
<body>

<script>
for (var i = 0; i <= 6; i++) {
    document.write(i + "<br>");
}
</script>

</body>
</html>
```

Result: We see the numbers from 0 the starting point to 6 listed.

```
0
1
2
3
4
5
6
```

Var i = 0: the variable named i starts at a value of 0.

i <= 6: for as long as it is less or equal to 6.

i++: incrementing **i** by 1.

Document.write(i + "<br>"): value of i on the page, <br> puts each value on a new line instead of getting them all on one horizontal line.

Code without <br> tag.

```
<script>
for (var i = 0; i <= 6; i++) {
    document.write(i);
}
</script>
```

Result: without the break tag, the values are all on one horizontal line.

```
0123456
```

Get to practice the code by changing values of *i*.

Another sample:

```
<script>
for (var i = 20; i <= 100; i += 20) {
    document.write(i + "<br>");
}
</script>
```

Result:

```
20
40
60
80
100
```

var i = 20 means that the start value of *i* is set to 20.

i <= 100 means for as long as *i* is less or equal to 100.

i += 20 means increment *i* by 20

Now let's use a decrement instead.

Sample:

```
<script>
for (var i = 15; i >= 0; i -= 3) {
    document.write(i + '<br>');
  }
</script>
```

Result: the loop counts from 15 to 0 with a decrement of 3.

```
15
12
9
6
3
0
```

If we use **i--** instead.

Sample:

```
<script>
for (var i = 5; i >= 0; i--) {
    document.write(i + '<br>');
  }
</script>
```

Result:

```
5
4
3
2
1
0
```

Note:

To put space before and after the operator is not required and is optional, **BUT** never put space between the two characters that form the operator such as:

Operator	Description
++	Means incrementing by 1
--	Means decrementing by 1
+=	Means incrementing by a defined amount
-=	Means decrementing by a defined amount
>=	Greater than or equal to
<=	Less than or equal to

2) JavaScript While loop:

There are two types of while loops, they repeat the line or lines of code more than one time and as long as the condition is true.

We have the condition which is an expression for the "as long as" condition that defines when to stop repeating the loop and the code to be executed with each pass through the loop.

a) **while loop:** block of code executed as long as the condition is true.

while (condition) {

block of code to be executed

```
}
```

Sample: The while loop loops as long as the condition is true.

Note: The variable used in the condition shall be increased to avoid the crash of the computer due to an ongoing loop that never ends.

```html
<body>

<p>To loop through a block of code as long as i < 9</p>
<button onclick="myFunction()">Click me</button>
<p id="test"></p>

<script>
function myFunction() {
    var x = "";
    var i = 3;
    while (i < 9) {
        x += "<br>The result is " + i;
        i++;
    }
    document.getElementById("test").innerHTML = x;
}
</script>
</body>
```

Result: it is good to practice the code by changing the *i* value and the *while* condition.

In our sample, the condition for looping is that the variable *i* must have a number less than 9, but *i* is already equal to 3 before the condition is assessed, the code inside the loop is jumped over and the execution is after the closing curly brace }.

To loop through a block of code as long as i < 9

Click me

The result is 3
The result is 4
The result is 5
The result is 6
The result is 7
The result is 8

b) *do/while loop:* executes the block of code at least once before the condition is checked to be true and even if it is false, then **repeats** it as long as the condition is **true**.

do {
   block of code to be executed
} while (condition);

Sample: the variable used in the condition must be incremented to stop the loop running forever.

```
<script>
function myFunction() {
    var x = "";
    var i = 3;
    do {
        x += "<br>The result is " + i;
        i++;
    }
    while (i < 9)
    document.getElementById("test").innerHTML = x;
}
</script>
```

Result: The loop will be executed at least once even with a false condition due to the execution of the block of code first before testing the condition.

The variable *i* has the value 3, so the execution continues with the *do* and the code to be executed inside the loop. Therefore code to be executed executes at least one time.

To loop through a block of code as long as i < 9

Click me

The result is 3
The result is 4
The result is 5
The result is 6
The result is 7
The result is 8

Another sample for do/while loop:

```
<body>
<script>
  do {
  //User to type his/her name.
    var name = prompt("Please type your name", "");
  //Ask again if box left empty.
  } while (name == null || name.length < 1)
//Reply Hi on the page.
document.write("Hi " + name);
</script>
</body>
```

Result: Because the script is right after the <body> tag, it will be executed once the page is opened, so the prompt box appears right way,

I used the IE browser, so the box appearance depends on the browser you are using but still a box appears anyway for the user to fill in his/her name. Try to close it or cancel it without typing anything, the box keeps coming back until you write something. Once done, click OK.

Note: in Google Chrome and Firefox browsers when cancel or close is clicked it returns *"Hi null"*.

IE (Internet Explorer) code output:

Once OK is clicked we get the Hi + name typed in the box.

Hi Sam

Note: We often use the prompt box to input a value before entering a page by using the *window.prompt ( )* method with the choice to drop the *window* prefix, its syntax is:

window.prompt("text of choice", "default text");

The first part of the prompt ( ) method *"text of choice"* is for instructions and the other one *"default text"* is a value already typed into the text box in our code it was an empty   string "" which leaves the text box empty.

The user gets a choice to either click "OK" after entering something or "cancel" to proceed. If *"cancel"* or *"close"* is clicked it returns *null.*

Google Chrome code output:

Result: once cancel is clicked it returns a value of *null*.

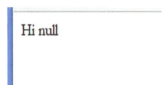

If OK is clicked without typing anything it retains the value " " which the empty string that has a 0 length. The box closes for a short time then pops right back again due to the condition on the *do* loop:

} while (name == null || name.length < 1)

Therefore the loop repeats if the name variable is equal to null, and if its length is less than 1, the prompt box will not stop coming back until something is entered in the box and the OK button has been clicked and all that mean the condition has been met.

If the user typed something, then once OK is clicked the variable gets it as value.

c) <u>Difference between the two loops:</u>

while the *do* loop for sure repeats the statement which is just the code at least once, the *while* loop might not because the decision is made at the beginning or start.

Important:

Ensure that condition eventually evaluates to false, if not the case then the loop never ends which is called an *infinite loop* in a sense that we will have to close the browser or use a new page. The target is to write the loop that repeats as many times as needed to perform the wanted task unlike the for loop that involves counting.

Big part of interactive apps and web pages. JavaScript offers other ways of decision making to whether or not repeat the loop and they are the *switch statement* and the *ternary operator* which involve writing codes to make decisions.

49- JavaScript Switch Statement:

Allows the execution and selection of a single block of statements from a group of possibilities. Acts like the if...else statement but offers a much shorter and easier syntax to use.

Syntax:

switch(expression) {
    case n1:
       code block to be executed
       break;
    case n2:
       code block to be executed
       break;

    ---
    default:
       default code block to be executed
}

The expression represents the name of a variable that contains a value such as the cases (n1, n2, and so forth). The --- means you can have more case statements. If a case match is detected the associated block of code is executed. The break statement sends execution past the bottom of the switch statement, the default block of code is optional and is the code to execute if and only if none of the other case statements are true.

50- The parseInt( ) Function in JavaScript:

Parses a string and returns an integer and if unable to convert the first character it returns NaN that stands for "Not-a-Number" value.

Sample code:

```
<head>
  <title>Switch statement sample code</title>
<script>
    function switchsample() {
  //value taken from the textbox.
    var number = parseInt(document.getElementById("textEntered").value)
  //Acknowledge info variable as string.
    var info = ""
    switch (number) {
      case 1:
        info = "one";
        break;
      case 2:
        info = "two"
        break;
      case 3:
        info = "three"
        break;

      default:
        info = "It has to be a number from 1 to 3.";
    }
  //Finding and generating outcome.
    document.getElementById("outcome").innerHTML = info;
    }
</script>
</head>
<body>
  <p>Enter a number from 1 to 3 then click the button:
  <input type="number" id="textEntered" style="width: 50px;" />
  <button onclick="switchsample()">
  ClickMe</button>
  </p>
  <p id="outcome" style="color:red;"></p>
</body>
```

Result 1: if a number from 1 to 3 is typed once you click the button that number shows up on the page.

Enter a number from 1 to 3 then click the button: 2   ⇕   ClickMe

two

Result 2: But if you type anything else a red sentence (because we styled in the code of outcome color to red) appears asking for a number between 1 and 3, see the Result 2 and the Result 3.

Enter a number from 1 to 3 then click the button: 5   ⇕   ClickMe

It has to be a number from 1 to 3.

Result 3:

Enter a number from 1 to 3 then click the button: Sam ⇕   ClickMe

It has to be a number from 1 to 3.

To explain the code process, after clicking the button, JavaScript switch statement decides what to output. The code has simple HTML and CSS elements to display the box, the button, a simple sentence that appears on the page located after the opening paragraph tag and the onclick event for the button that has the JavaScript function *switchsample( )* which is right after the <script> open tag and if called the *var number* code is executed first, once the variable is created and any value entered in the box by the user will be put in, the *parseInt( )* method converts the info entered to a number and if something else was typed instead it returns *NaN* that stands for "Not a Number".

Then comes the *var info = " "* code with an empty string.

After that come the 3 cases with the one, two and three values, if none of the three cases is true then the default case takes over and state *"It has to be a number from 1 to 3."*.

In a way the *switch statement* works exactly like the *if...else* statements and it is fine to replace the case statement by the *if....else* statement, we get the same result.

Same sample code but using *if...else* statements instead of *switch statement.*

```
<script>
    function switchsample() {
//value taken from the textbox.
  var number = parseInt(document.getElementById("textEntered").value)
//Acknowledge info variable as string.
    var info = ""

        if (number == 1) {
            info = "one";
} else if (number == 2) {
            info = "two";
} else if (number == 3) {
            info = "three";
} else {
    info = "It has to be a number from 1 to 3.";
}
//Finding and generating outcome.
        document.getElementById("outcome").innerHTML = info;
}
</script>
</head>
<body>
  <p>Enter a number from 1 to 3 then click the button:
  <input type="number" id="textEntered" style="width: 50px;" />
  <button onclick="switchsample()">
  ClickMe</button>
  </p>
  <p id="outcome" style="color:red;"></p>
</body>
```

Result:

Enter a number from 1 to 3 then click the button: 1   ClickMe

one

51- JavaScript Ternary Operator:

Called the *conditional operator* and used for an understood *if* decisions offering an abbreviated notation, it assigns a value to a variable according to a defined condition, while the switch statement is based on many choices to make a decision.

Syntax:

variable name = (condition) ? Value1 (if true):value2(if false)

The condition evaluates to true or false, to *value1* if the condition is *true* and to *value2* if the condition is *false*.

Sample:

```
<body>
<p>Enter your age then click the button:</p>
<input id="age" value="22" />

<button onclick="myFunction()">GO</button>
<p id="test"></p>

<script>
function myFunction() {
 var age,driving;
 age = document.getElementById("age").value;
 driving = (age < 16) ? "Cannot drive":"Can drive";
 document.getElementById("test").innerHTML = driving + " the car.";
}
</script>
</body>
```

Result 1:

Enter your age then click the button:

22   GO

Can drive the car.

Result 2:

Enter your age then click the button:

| 13 | | GO |

Cannot drive the car.

First the code starts with a variable named *age* and another one named *driving* which starts with a condition of age less than 16 followed by the ? (question mark), the value1 is the string *"cannot drive"* and the value2 is the string *"can drive"*.

If the age entered in the box is less than 16 the outcome reads *cannot drive*, if the number entered is => (equal or greater) than 16 the outcome will read *can drive*.

The *ternary operator* does what *if* statement does.

Sample: The *if* statement.

```
<script>
function myFunction() {
  var age,driving;
  age = document.getElementById("age").value;
  if (age < 16) {
    driving = "Cannot drive";
} else {
    driving = "Can drive";
}
  document.getElementById("test").innerHTML = driving + " the car.";
}
</script>
```

Result:

Enter your age then click the button:

| 18 | | GO |

Can drive the car.

52- Summary:

An *array* is just a list of variables that we get hold of through a number, *loops* are for repeating the line or lines of code many times until it meets a specific condition and the *switch statement* and *ternary operators* provide an alternative way for decision-making.

53- Timers and Transitions:

53a- Introduction:

Timers are JavaScript events, usually we like things to speed up and not slow down but the one exception is transition effect where slowing down is necessary so people can catch the change happening at a slow motion. We can do that with JavaScript timers, however, CSS3 provides transitions which offer the control of time with the possibility of slowing down things, in this way we are not completely dependent on JavaScript for animation effects.

53b- Timers or Timing Events:

Allow code execution time delay, JavaScript waits before executing some function, the code will be executed at a precised time intervals called timing events.

there are two ways of using timers:

1) **setTimeout( ):** The parentheses hold the *function* that executes once and the *milliseconds* which is a precised number of seconds.

2) **setInterval( ):** The parentheses hold the *function* that executes in a repetitive way at a precised time intervals expressed in *milliseconds* similar to a loop but with a time delay.

Note: *setTimeout( )* and *setInterval( )* **are methods** of HTML DOM (Document Object Model).

The function is a JavaScript function to be execute and a millisecond is $1/1000^{th}$ of a second.

setTimeout( ) and *setInterval( )* are methods of the window event, they might be written with window and dot such as *window.setInterval( )* and *window.setTimeout( )* which is left out in JavaScript so it is OK to just use *setInterval( ) and setTimeout( ).*

3) Syntax to assign a variable name to a timer:

var name = setTimeout("JavaScript function", delay in milliseconds);

var name = setInterval("JavaScript function", delay in milliseconds);

You can choose the name of the variable, the code using *setInterval( )* works the same as *setTimeout( ),* once the timer is connected with a variable name you are able to stop it by using:

clearInterval(variable name of the timer) **Or** *clearTimeout(variable name of the timer).*

setInterval( ) **code samples:**

Sample 1: Setting the execution time interval.

```
<!DOCTYPE html>
<html>
<body>
<p>The alert box will continue to open every 5 seconds.</p>
<p>Close the window to stop the ongoing alert box.</p>

<button onclick="setInterval(function(){
             alert('How are you?')},5000);">Click</button>
</body>
</html>
```

Result:

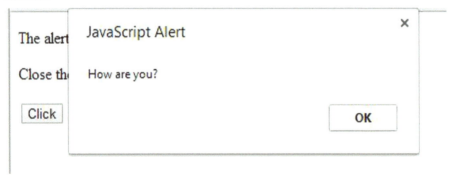

Note:

Each time you close the alert box, after 5 seconds it opens again, so you need to close the browser window.

Sample 2: Using the *setInterval( )* method to display the current time every 3 seconds.

```
<body>
<p id="test"></p>
<script>
var clock=setInterval(function(){currentTime()},3000);

function currentTime() {
var date = new Date();
document.getElementById("test").innerHTML =
                              date.toLocaleTimeString();
}
</script>
</body>
```

Result: After 7:02:01 PM comes 7:02:04 PM then 7:02:07 PM and so on, every 3 seconds.

7:02:01 PM

Note: The seconds part of the displayed time will execute every 3 seconds and display multiples of 3.

Try to change the time to 5000 which is 5 seconds or any number you want.

<u>Conclusion</u>

Learning JavaScript, which is a scripting language, its basics and fundamentals is very easy and helpful to start learning a compiled programming languages which is more complex.